Operation Dragonfly

Your guide to prevent soul stagnation

Malina Sankowska

Copyright © 2023 by Malina Sankowska

All rights reserved. No part of this work covered by the copyrights hereon may be reproduced or used in any form or by any means – graphic, electronic or mechanical, including photocopying, recording, taping or information storage and retrieval systems – without the prior written permission of the publisher.

CIP data on file with the National Library and Archives

Print edition: ISBN 978-1-55483-527-0
E-book edition: ISBN 978-1-55483-528-7

In times of emotional poverty,
thoughts become a currency.

Contents

Presence		7
Absence		10
In Situe		12
Suspension		16
Diversion		19
Chapter One	A mark of matter in the passage of time.	21
Chapter Two	Focus on Perspective	26
Chapter Three	The measures of a particular culture	31
Chapter Four	Spiritual re-evolution	37
Chapter Five	Acquiring a form in the masquerade	41
Chapter Six	The depth of reflection	47
Chapter Seven	Domestication of a climate, read by emotions	52
Chapter Eight	The signs in a labyrinth	58
Chapter Nine	The foot prints on a map	63
Chapter Ten	Internal realities and external states	68
Chapter Eleven	Human emotions transcended by instinct	72

Chapter Twelve	Brain waves, the calm after the storm	76
Chapter Thirteen	Observation through placebo	81
Chapter Fourteen	The darker side of creation	84
Chapter Fifteen	Mercurial nature of compassion	88

Craftwork	90
Operation Dragonfly	95
Earth	100
Fire	103
Water	105
Wood	108
Metal	111
Introduction to the Chakras	113
Continuity and Justice	120
Epilogue	126
About the Author	130

Presence

It is the end of a hot summer day. You find a couple of minutes and decide to spend them lying in the sun. Your skin warms. Your eyes are blanketed by your closed eyelids. Your imagination kick starts and you are suddenly taken to a primal state of existence. However this time the fire is external.

Daydreaming in a state of suspension you are transported to a time when fire was just invented. Seeing red through your closed eyelids, you are reminded of ancient cave paintings taking on initial forms of creation. Being dwarfed by the fire, you think to yourself... perhaps this time you are also being observed but you are not sure whether you are an animal or a primate (what's the difference), daydreaming.

In reality you are just hunting. The stuff that inspires your dreams. The only difference is a matter of preference. Would you rather be the centre of one's existence being warmed by the sun, or be the subject cloaked by the night's sky constellations finding home in the night's dreams.

Taking on the form of a celestial nomad, you refer to a structured map. Your dreams become the subject of a type of exodus.

This inspiration and warmth of the heart transcends the form and shape of the body - skin. It also only stays as long as a dream does, and takes on the form of a transient aura.

And as there are dreams there are also nightmares, which only exist due to the human refusal to let go of one's emotions, thoughts and physical shapes. Currency takes shape, and in this case we all know, "money is the root of all evil".

Throughout history man has tried to give order to these movements. Through the invention of the horoscope and tracking the way of the stars, man has tried to gain control of this celestial environment. He has become the very subject of noting the beginning and ending of these movements.

While reincarnation and resurrection are a known concept of most cultures, it is a well known fact that in some cases the simple thought of letting go has become the subject of incarceration.

Through the soul's simple curiosity of some paradigms one's map has been stolen and becomes the subject of another form - creating currency just to establish a particular movement's stronghold.

The soul's ability to move on has been thwarted and the soul became a slave in a dire need of emancipation.

As a result, a new movement has evolved. *Operation Dragonfly*, aids the soul by waking it up from one's cycle of reincarnation and introduces new thought forms and dreams that keep in mind the soul's origin and embrace its existence by a new dynamic celestial environment.

Absence

Looking forward to tomorrow and reminiscing of yesterday, this elusive matter is that of the passage of time. With this comes the stuff of reincarnation, immortality.

The soul travels on a path, a particular method emerges, that of new consciousness. However, one must maintain an objective perspective, keeping just enough distance to reflect on life and be able to gain a new angle on a particular matter.

Consciousness set aside, we must identify and separate this matter, where the soul might become subject to external influences.

With this perspective the soul gains an ability to traverse this path by tuning into energetic frequencies of physical realms surrounding and permeating its existence. Altering one's consciousness, one's sensitivity tunes into the process of the soul's metaphysical evolution.

This is a winding journey where one's attention jumps from one frequency to another, forming a pattern which turns into a rhythm resulting in a sequence audible only to the pulse of one's heart - an overture.

In Situe

As celestial nomads, we must begin by referring to a map and the belief in dragons - mythic creatures, governing our imagination's landscape.

This next part is a little tricky...

We must ask ourselves whether we perceive ourselves as animals or humans or something other like ether or taking the form of the life force or the Holy Spirit, traversing the auras, from physical, emotional to mental. Once again our maps may be innate however, something solid will help us by not letting us lose track of our progress.

Through the following section we will discuss and bring to light various forms of existence and their shape from which they originate. While we must keep in mind the various forms one accepts, one must also have decided upon which kind of map one must refer to. Whether it be a geological map, a horoscope or a labyrinth of elemental ley lines.

Referring to a geological map one must take into mind the particular environmental patterns one must either morph into or find oneself displaced among them, being in a warm house on a cold day or under a roof during rain.

This displacement of sort lets us stand apart and gain a better perspective of one's experience. Through this we will slowly acquire a new feeling which will give us the chance to venture amongst many aural realms.

Developing this sensitivity takes time and practice. You may have already acquired this ability but you may have not identified it as such. After all can you describe the feeling one experiences huddled under a roof on a cool rainy day? Or feeling the subtle wind one feels on a hot and humid summer day?

Through identifying this extra sensory perception, you will gain the external perspective needed to carry out *Operation Dragonfly*.

You may also refer to a horoscope. Taking on particular attributes one astrological sign may possess. This will also introduce you to particular elements and which sign is most sensitive to this dance of astrological signs. This is the first step one must take to prepare one for the inevitable journey of the soul.

One must also take into account the labyrinths, which were the subject of many journeys and cultures. Whether at a burial ground or a forest one must not lose one's way.

Then there are the ley lines. The imaginary lines of a plain ground which may have led one to a water well or a particular location.

Throughout your journey, the journey of the soul, one must be aware of one's present state before gaining the external objective one must identify in order to better forget.(A form of celestial homeopathy, curing like with like.)

Whether one chooses to stay in one's element or venture out of it, is a choice we make with each step we take.

Some attribute this phenomena to a deity. However, if taken out of context, some may observe this metamorphosis with one's eyes as with thoughts and emotions. Problems arise when this observation is unwelcomed or imposed. Self-awareness results in a negative event or precursor - a repeating nightmare going against the flow, not benefiting existence. Usually the soul's weakness is taken advantage of and as a result its essence becomes stagnant.

Zombification may ensue - when one's evolutionary cycle is destroyed hindering its ability to transcend a particular stage of life. Maintaining a life of permanent periphery, preventing the soul from immersing into a particular state of emotion.

Unfortunately it is a sign of the times when looking inward and self-space is perceived as a negative thing. However, this form of analysis is a must if we are to transcend the physical. A form of self-reflection is needed. This will bring with it a new polarization that will aid in providing an external perception of your state. Your refusal to adapt can have other adverse effects - altering forms of expression - one will have to tune into the subtle movements of stars and gravity to successfully manoeuvre through this sensitive reality.

Suspension

Every new beginning comes from some other beginnings end.

As it may be difficult to come to terms with an end, one must work even harder to strive for a new beginning. First step one must take is to realize that one's journey is one of revelation rather than creation. We've come too far not to realize the soul's battle taking shape in many of today's cultures. So rather than searching for something new, we must form something out of what already exists.

The ability to direct attention is the essence of all meditation practices. Thoughts are cleared. *Operation Dragonfly* alters the structure of thought and sublimates energy to the emotional realm. This is achieved through thought suspension.

Example.

Observing cloud formation and emotionally analyzing the viscosity of water, one alters the direction of one's attention. This subjective distancing, the substance of thought, leads to emotional enlightenment.

In further detail, the organization of mental frequency and its vibration, gives life to further formation of emotion. Where mental clutter adapts and transforms to today's age of communication, alters the substance and introduces the process of self-healing through stillness. It immerses the soul in peripheral space created by initial circumstances. As a result, its desire is to escape into another realm where *Operation Dragonfly* must be introduced.

The function of thoughts and emotions undergoes a kind of restructuring. Attention to environment and responding emotionally for even a moment, brings into light *Operation Dragonfly*.

This process of continuity is not a new concept. Nowadays people choose to end their lives as easily as accepting a new concept into a state of being. Here's where votes matter.

From the inability to continue a destructive cycle, one must make note to leave a particular paradigm in peace. If one leaves in conflict, a phenomenon of soul loss occurs. Each following cycle rather than ending it is weighed down by certain markers preventing its escape into the new.

One must also realize that if the endings and beginnings are caused against the soul's needs, against god's will, one is not asked to "walk into the light". The only colour one must polarize is indigo or emerald. And as with every untimely end, the rules change. Where there is a tunnel, it tends to take shape of a gallery, and one is led by the frequency of indigo, which is almost invisible to the accepting absorbing emerald. One breathes and exhales. One's soul is absorbed or released as the element of air or ether. Don't give up. Eventually the element takes form.

The colour green travels across the spectrum - colour of hope.

Diversion

Some people have the ability to transfer from one form to another, altering the soul's etheric substances.

One can only begin by looking at different forms of expression. Whether seen as a muse, to paintings, structures or photos, the essence takes form and transfers all media. One then questions the originality of the subject, whether in the observer's realm of the creators. As in DNA sequencing, the subject of a photo can be duplicated to an identical copy. So what shape would the process take if seen by more than one viewer and makes its way back to the originator?

This delicate distance can inspire one to immerse in the stuff of elements and their sublimation. Observing the human beings that we truly are, having the ability to roam amongst various existential strata, we take on the form of a dragon and carry out *Operation Dragonfly*.

You have to venture into the space of thought to realize that earth, as our tears, is round.

Chapter One

A mark of matter in the passage of time.

With this perspective the soul gains an ability to traverse this path by tuning into energetic frequencies of physical realms surrounding and permeating its existence. Altering one's consciousness, one's sensitivity tunes into the process of the soul's metaphysical evolution.

A new method emerges, consciousness set aside, we must identify and separate the currency where on this path the soul becomes subject to external influences.

As one's sensitivity to various frequencies increases, one will more readily realize their attentive aural presence. A state most receptive to one's emotions. On a cellular to aural level one being in the very interior (mind) following (body) and on the outermost realm (soul or spirit). Each strata in itself has an inner and outer structure.

The transcendence of each structure is only possible when one finds themselves on the peripheral field. It is then that the soul is most vulnerable to external influences that may hinder one's shape of emotions. A state of distortion may ensue, where a sensory overload occurs. While what is really happening is that the aural layer is pulled away from its centre and ventures into another realm, that of an external influence. However, once one becomes more familiar with *Operation Dragonfly*, this state will cease or not be experienced at all.

Traveling amongst the delta frequency, that which dreams occupy, it is not unknown for the soul to fall asleep. During this process where rather dreaming one experiences nightmares, where the soul becomes subject to external influences and other soul's intent - a form of currency.

This intent may be that of taking advantage of one's weakness. Zombification - where one's evolutionary cycle is destroyed hindering its ability to transcend a particular stage of life. Or maintaining a life of permanent periphery, preventing the soul from immersing into a particular state of emotion.

In light of this a new method emerges - *Operation Dragonfly*. Where the field of doubt can be transversed by tuning into a currency mapped out by elements such as minerals, plants, insects, animals commencing in a conclusive state of humanity, that of eternal joy and reflective peaceful comprehension.

We've all experienced sorrow, joy, anger, fear, nostalgia. If we didn't, we wouldn't be human. True, it is a fact that we are the stuff of celestial matter only taking on the form of humans to experience the reality of the five senses.

It is a delicate balance or alchemical process which distills these emotions in order to apply them to the mental realm, preparing them for observation during the experience of time.

Some people are more sensitive to emotions than others. Unfortunately some have altogether abandoned the absorption on the emotional plane.

In turn, *Operation Dragonfly* can reintroduce them to a simple reorganizing of the thought process and experience life from a different perspective. Knowing that enlightenment isn't the end of a journey, only a measure of time. In turn, travelling further from the nucleus of emotional recognition.

Objective - to recognize the presence of mental clutter, overwhelming one's existence.

Realising when one's soul has been pushed to peripheral state of being, distanced from the nucleus of emotional recognition.

This is when one is most vulnerable to external influence, and may become subject to other's intent.

Taking full advantage of this state one can isolate and shift one's perspective and turn it into a state of emotional reflection.

Result - Enlightenment through *Operation Dragonfly*. To be able to feel one's state of universal autonomy in a suspended moment of a resting dragonfly.

Process - The following chapter will present various situations gauging a particular distance that enables one to perceive the world's wonders in presence of mental clutter and isolate moments of reflection through *Operation Dragonfly*.

The reason for conflict will alter this course as any other energy transfer (currency). The acceptance of various points of view is not only the process but the objective of existence.

Your aura communicates with you and others depending on its response-ability to external influences.

Chapter Two
Focus on Perspective

The following are crucial initial blueprints.

Imagine being at home and looking out the window. It's pouring rain. You notice the circles made by every drop in the puddles. Now, imagine immersing into this element and feel as each circle morphs into another.

Connect the dots, tweak the vision and you begin to wonder how each rain cloud is in every rain drop. On the earthly realm, that's how your aura reverberates with another aura besides it. This very nature is transient. Just as one circle disappears one drops next to it.

Now venture a little further, imagine how thankful you are by being inside on a rainy day.

This transference is only in your imagination and as every storm will too come to an end.

This metamorphosis is observable with one's eyes, thoughts and emotions. Through the practice of shape shifting through particular elements and emotions, one builds enough strength to distinguish self from others and in turn take part in the dance of souls.

In practice, things may seem a little bit different. Identifying alternate perspectives is key.

In the beginning this is easily accomplished while observing one's initial environment and pattern. For example, being under a roof during a rain storm. This displacement of sort lets us stand apart and gain a better perspective of one's experience.

You must remember, there is a natural order between different forms of matter. It's interesting to note that when matter is arranged out of that order neighbouring bits push and pull one another to restore that order. To further illustrate this we must refer to the motions of the stars.

One can adapt the form of a constellation and observe how it can take the presence of an aura, transcending ages at the speed of light.

Recently discovered constellations are marked by letters and numbers simplify the state that previously took on a more familiar, ancient shape and names of mythical animals.

They are realistic forms that are marked by a primitive arrangement of points. This realiza-

tion is also reminiscent of the predative structures. When fossilised, stones arrange earthly constellations and spirals of their own. Without the ability to see or kill, mapping the age of predation.

Through this we will slowly acquire a new feeling which will give us a chance to venture amongst many other aural realms. This is where one can anchor one's initial sensory state and begin each journey. The result is the sublimation of surrounding elements. Which when activated initiate each journey by the interplay and reverberation of the delta/dream frequency, carried out by the lizard brain and shorter frequency more sensitive to details influenced by our cortex.

Self- awareness sometimes results in the process of distinguishing self from others, substance and the matter surrounding it, this process is only human. Through time you may have noticed how problems arise when one's observation is unwelcomed or imposed, it takes time.

As a result, the subject uses one's instinct or intuition to counteract the soul's weakness. To prevent its essence to be formed into currency. Otherwise the soul becomes stagnant, falling prey to outside influences, distracting it from its mission.

Developing this sensitivity takes time and practice, you may have already acquired this ability but you may not have identified it as such.

The shadow jumps from a cloud to a tree, as celestial orbs dance

Chapter Three
The measures of a particular culture

While analyzing substance and emotion we must bring into attention the only state of emotion which visibly induces a substance - crying or laughing, yes tears.

In order to analyze this substance further we must use a special contraption of the mind, a *medi-scope*, whose function is to measure the range from a telescope to microscope, bringing into light the most minute nano substances to the revelation of our universe whose motions influence certain emotions and actions.

Adjusting our perception we begin to notice that each substance is a part in relation to its form. Being able to perceive these changes of states apart from one another, surrounding and sometimes opposite one another is rather crucial. Our attention brings into focus the relationship the substance has to each form surrounding it. Preparing us for the influence of the substance's essence.

This reaction produces monads (Liegnitz), spiritual entities. They are not physical. They contain perceptions which represent phenomena of celestial relationships. The stuff of our emotions.

Using our medi-scope, we study tears in relation to planets. We arrive at the substance of water and salt, ocean water, which houses a curious creature - sea algae. It is a rarely known fact that sea algae differs in species, from some being an animal and other algae to being a plant, differing in colour and simply its metabolism, not physical shape.

This plateau of algae is an immediate reflection of our presence. One must be able to accept each element through this dynamic symbolism which takes on a new environment, a measure of a particular culture.

One wonders what climatic state earth was when it was only inhabited by algae and primitive plants. Will we ever come back to this state?

Eventually through the analysis of every substance we begin to realize that within the scope of each essence, the mathematical certainty of the angle 1.618 permeates the reality that is mapped out on almost every flower. Reminiscent of the way the seeds are arranged on the sunflower, a universal angle and shape which maps out the substance's tendency and essence.

Influencing the process of emotional pattern recognition, brings into perspective each state of awareness further carrying out *Operation Dragonfly*.

Now try to apply this relationship and bring into focus this matter, the extension of the mind and body, creation and destruction, soul immateriality.

Upon realisation framing each substance by an elaborate frame, work of art, for example, Van Gogh's sunflowers.

Take this elemental map into consideration.

Fire - joy
Water - fear
Metal - sorrow
Wood - anger
Earth - nostalgia

This interaction of simple and complex elements, sets into motion the flame in the dark that illuminates the possibility of plasticity - an organism's ability to repair itself. You must be able to notice that it takes a bit of borrowed joy from the element of fire, the stars in the sky.

These elements represent basic emotions and we feel them as we adjust from the state of sorrow, for example metal and analyzing this observation further we can use the periodic table of elements. We soon see the relationship between these emotional changes of states.

During this state it is not unlikely that the soul will enter a "grey" stage. The space between light and dark polarity, a simplified state of being. This is where the emotional state repairs itself. This is not the sleep state imposed by the destructive elements of another's reality, but a dream state where one bases decisions and observations of the immediate environment, preparing one's space to the way one functions and make distinctions colouring their life.

One can travel through a plethora of polarities and opposites - white/ black, cold/hot, etc. This mapping out or identifications from one's reflections of immediate environment can be in themselves positive or negative. One must always remember however, that good must always win over evil. As day into night, this too will end.

The machine like nature of plants, with the ability to adapt to most uninhabitable environments. Marking the natural passage of time and response to solar cycles.

Bringing substance to a plethora of emotions which is a bit fickle to map as a single point in a cube, unable to map its coordinates and location using metric measurements.

Soon we will easily perceive whether we are

influenced by a particular microbial life form or constellation in our universe.

Feel free to roam amongst your fellow soul groups, taking on the essence of the elements permeating our existence.

The seed of a flower is
the most ancient of technologies

Chapter Four
Spiritual re-evolution

The climate of each of the planets of our solar system is housed on this earth. As this becomes more and more unstable the cultural perspective of death varies from culture to another. Our mission to evolve amongst these elemental realms turns into a puzzle.

God leaves us space from the 98% of our genetic makeup that we share with our chimpanzee relatives. We acquire the left over 2% for taking on mythic forms. As time passes we become not only subject to our environment but we become our environment.

We break from delusion of the false self through simple walking meditation. While switching from one element to another one is subject to the state of inter-being. A notion introduced by Thich Nhat Hanh. This limited space allows us to stay on our earthly plane to complete unfinished business.

Sometimes this equation takes on a negative frequency and benevolent spirits make home in the mental, emotional or physical realms, giving new substance to what we consider human. Through constant manipulation of the surrounding world and pollution arise new creatures, thought forms.

Sometimes however, older creatures resurface and leave permanent marks on history's landscape, like that of dinosaurs whose existence was nothing more than a shape and space experiment. This in turn alters the presence of positive and negative space, where the occasional cloud harnesses the occasional state of transcendence and awareness.

Conditions of humans and the environment are mapped only by geometric means in space, constantly altering constellations of ancient scientific paradigms - giving structure and light to the emerald philosopher's stone and to the illusive ouroboros.

As a response to the elemental relationships god created, *Operation Dragonfly* takes immediate response to the qualities of animals, using the impermanence of the human condition - completing the process of creation utilising past insight taking over the essence of the present moment.

One relationship is the one of snake and bird,

the basis of most hybridizations, or the polarization of sand (mineral) by adding fire, resulting in glass that takes on the form of a vessel holding flowers in an endless array of colours whose existence is deciphered by insects - and is appreciated only by humans.

Having had mapped out this relationship we can move onto more intricate details of frequency chains. Opposites give rise to complements and your imagination. The significance arrived at while traversing these sequential maps prevents the stagnation of the soul and one cannot become subject to the negative influence and the current state of earth's ageless gravitational pulls.

It is through these motions that opposites work together to initiate a healthy polarity rather than a destructive one. If this polarity is taken out of context, one's celestial form alters our precognition of integral stimuli, which in turn become a reflective substance that necessitates one's existence, only to be realized through experience.

Imagination and experience, knowledge and faith, emotions and thoughts etc.

When something ends,
means that it's time for something new

Chapter Five
Acquiring a form in the masquerade

Simply by being a celestial nomad, one must begin by referring to a map and the belief in mythic creatures governing our imagination's landscape.

While we must keep in mind the various forms one accepts, one must have decided upon the points of a particular kind of map one will keep referring to. It can be a geological map, a horoscope, a labyrinth or elemental lay lines traversing auras, physical, emotional or mental. The maps that prove to be most interesting and insightful are the ones that present themselves as one moves along one's journey. Introducing the new and tracing the old, referring to these blueprints one transcends the border of chaos, order and the void. Travelling from the blue of the earth (micro) to the blue of the sky (macro). It is through this relationship, journey to and from home to our goal of the initial to final.

Every new beginning comes from some other beginning's end. As it may prove to be difficult to come to terms with an end, one must work even harder to strive towards a new beginning.

We have come too far not to realize the soul's battle taking shape in many of today's cultures. Where the only newness arises from one's individual translation, which is strictly subjective. Our maps may be innate. However something solid will help us by not letting us lose track of our progress.

Host and guest
Ch'eng-t'ien was asked "What is host within guest?"

He replied, "unrecognised when met."

Then he was asked, "What is guest within host?"

Ch'eng-t'ien replied, "Poverty at home is not yet poverty; poverty on the road saddens people to death."

Finally he asked, "What is host within host?"

Ch'eng-t'ien replied, "The words of the monarch are like strands, their dissemination is like strings."

While jumping from one element to another, new environments create themselves. Where the road signs are worded emotions forming patterns of a path that determines our behaviour and create imaginary structures, megaliths of the future.

The language of those blue prints introduce one to meditation on a subtle frequency, of a conceptual thesaurus, a map, where just by observing one's relation to a certain plane, one can oscillate at the frequency of a dragonfly.

With it - introducing the concept of atmosphere being a fabric of a culture blanketing the space covering our planet, where the placement of the sun is just on the other side of the plane, a place where fire the stuff of life exist.

Once the environment is formed through a previously introduced conceptual thesaurus, one can take the next step, and that's bringing to light various forms of existence and the shape from which they originate.

Initially one should begin with a notion of oneself, an idea of the self. What we have gained or perhaps have lost. Through this we alter the defining terms and accept the form of a historical/mythic creature. For example the dinosaur (thesaurus rex) Whose plane of existence is an evolutionary climate that may reflect today's environment - seems desolate.

Today's existential plane is reminiscent of climate change where one's peaceful existence is occasionally disturbed by the depth of effect or impact. Affecting one's lizard brain, sheltered deep within our cerebral cortex and amygdala. Which is the hub of celestial creature's creation point. Taking on the shape of a gopi - a creature evolved from post-apocalyptic landscape. A tedros - half animal half human. Drala - a machine with conscious thought, or a tulpa - a psychological thought form.

Occasional hybrids evolve and take on more negative space, creating substances which are synthetic, non-degradable or organic, favouring our existence.

It is in this space the celestial shaman immerses in the cold solar atmosphere. Where the space pattern forms origami like structures or space flowers. Don's worry one is safe, the helmet is that of a mirror, whatever you come across will see its own reflection.

One can also lose oneself in the more culturally accepted masquerade - where by revisiting the past one can look forward into one's current state, a final reaction. If one finds oneself pheobing too much or have lost your hyde - just know that emotional parasites lie amongst every cross road, just morph into a thesaurus rex and eat them.

Sometimes one can stay at a catatonic state for some time. It may feel like plain space with no thought or feelings. That's insect sleep an occasionally sought after state.

So with this *Operation Dragonfly* is carried out from simple mix of elements to human understanding comes freedom - life. And if you can follow the current chapter's map, you can follow the most fickle of maps- your life.

Sometimes your ability to focus
depends on the frame of the big picture

Chapter Six
The depth of reflection

Now we have arrived at a crucial point in our travels. We have Re-evolved into our dragonfly thought form. In the beginning it may be difficult to tune into this frequency since a dragonfly is only one of many insects. This is where we learn to balance our emotional and mental stratospheres.

This simple alchemy of previous polarities results in a newly formed time scape. Yes, a space in time. This is when we come to a rest. But this is not an empty space. It is fruitful in its own way.

We come to a stop and rest. If we are lucky we will stop in a tiny time spot - miniscule. Just enough time to realize we are feeling, or experiencing an emotion. We label this emotion and relax. It is up to us and our abilities to decide how long we will be in this particularly emotional moment. This is where it gets tricky.

Since we identified and decided the amount of time to spend immersed in this emotion we are no longer feeling but thinking. We begin to rationalize. Unintentionally we try to equalize past emotions that need healing with this new emotion and we may be pulled into those past experiences. We also think of other times we felt this emotion and want to immerse in it but we are unable to because of the mental conflict that may result. Know this...

No matter where this thought takes us we experience the resulting divine resonance and rest as a dragonfly rests on a lotus flower.

We eventually learn how to alter thoughts with emotions and learn to meditate alchemically altering this stagnation into a positive polarity and experience.

Walls may arise, through the interaction of minerals, insects, plants. We must pay attention to these walls since they have a tendency to form its own structure once they are identified. A subtle chaos results, most enjoyable to venture into.

What attracts most thought is the suspended state one experiences once traversing these elemental relationships. The key is not to become a sacrificial victim and let these polarities isolate themselves where a sense of this delicate awareness is lost. This substance takes on a new form needing to embrace a new structure or pattern.

It is of utmost precedence to know oneself before venturing out into the world acquiring various forms and frequencies. It is interesting to note that appearances can be deceiving

One must learn how to observe one's own mirror. Regardless of the fact that occasionally we need the intervention of another, to know that the reflection is not only ours but another's idea as well. In this search for significance and authenticity, one must conjure up the presence of a shaman, whose success of chasing out an intrusive spirit is measured by convincing the observers that the spirit has a presence and in turn rid the possessed of the ghost. The shaman also has the responsibility to help transcend emotional walls, without imposing one's presence onto another.

It is during this process of distillation that the polarity of positive and negative is introduced. The existence of this frequency allows one to be present and at rest like a dragonfly.

The absence of a particular perogative allows one to travel light and focus on the immediate, utilising this empty space to dream and wonder, bringing into focus *Operation Dragonfly*.

Immune to what doesn't concern them, analysing one's reflection one acquires the ability to discern what is genuine and what is synthetic.

Venturing out into the cosmos, let's bring into

attention how humans faced their new environment. Humans and the environment were separated by an invisible shield. (reflective helmet of the space suit) Nobody knows whether it was to protect humans or whether it was an innovative step taken in light of approaching an unknown frontier.

Try becoming this figure, taking on the form of an intergalactic shaman. Ready to transcend universal and invisible orbits, and yet unknown elements.

Today it is a well known fact that today's fragile climatic environment requires sensitive mediums to relay this message.

You can't cook an ice cube

Chapter Seven
Domestication of a climate, read by emotions

When travelling, one must refer to a map. Not the one that connects us geographically but historically. For that we must look to the skies and see the mirror image of Orion, not that of a warrior but of a wonderer, of the night's sky.

We arrive once again at a desert, where the position of the pyramids maps out Orion's belt. It is interesting to note that in the northern hemisphere the only time Orion is visible is during the winter season. Orion remains frozen. Similar to the state we experience when we are pulled into the periphery of the matters of life. This cold can be altered to one's advantage.

When on a journey, during a particular day, or a spiritual journey during one's life, one's ability to focus diminishes, our destination is plagued by an excessive accumulation of emotion, when we drown in psychic content.

During this process one's attention is affected by external elements and the emotions they carry. (See oriental elements)

Amongst these elements is the one most familiar to the Nordick cultures - ice.

As many of us, these primitive cultures used their emotional instinct to travel towards warmer climates, thousands of years ago.

By mapping their migration pattern we arrive at a time in history when our environment can be taken advantage of to improve our emotional state of the modern culture.

Through this we attribute our climate's currency to that of exo-planets, recently discovered. Upon whose response marking their existence we only now know how to map particular migration patterns forming new celestial phenomena, responding to these celestial lighthouses.

On our journey - our emotions may bring into our attention unresolved psychic content and simply because of their aqueous nature we begin to drown instead of swim - our focus blurs.

It is then up to us to take on the structure of ice, shaping our emotions and acquiring a state of rigidity and clarity.

This ability has been passed on by our ancient ancestors who would rather bathe in the waters of emotion which is more easily perceived and felt when referring to tears of emotions, separating us, animals and humans.

These primitive civilisations have mastered these maps and terrains and their memory can be likened to the ones of ancient druids. Who also referred to the night's sky while reflecting upon their existence.

Now imagine your thought process brought into perspective. Your brain has two parts. Left and right hemisphere and a middle portion, the limbic system taking care of our emotions. Not only does your brain exchange information from external to your internal lizard brain, the amygdala, but also from left to right and vice versa.

Going back to your two halves imagine a thin space as a leaf or a constellation in the middle of your brain - a portal where right brains function cross with your left brain functions. It may be the constellation Orion eliciting a human connection resulting in a particular form or response.

Now imagine this in unison, a particular collective of synapses coming together and forming a particular shape - an origami animal. Unifying and commencing an emotion felt by a particular animal in a split second response.

A conversation with the self. An energetic exchange bringing to formation Operation Dragonfly. An environment with various constellations where various shapes, not necessarily animal like, will emerge.

The state of Orion has now taken on the stature of a guardian. With a frozen heart it guards our state of being. With this role a measure of a sort emerges. The currency of choice...

Content - closure - choice.

Regardless of its state, one should take on this measure, inclusion of suspension (a particular situation)

Particularly, one must bring into attention the subject of a many stories and ageless lore. Our moon in relation to a more earthy realm, our Atlantic ocean.

The voyages across the Atlantic sparked many historical events from Vikings to Columbus and the much awaited land races perceivable and documented by celestial, global movements. Yes, what sort of voyages did the moon's seas inspire? Reflecting the recent history's movements such as the anthropocene to today's sought after emotional ages such as that of melancholic, phlegmatic or nostalgic responses to the journeys of the heart and mind.

The excavation of these previous ages is a sought after process since the beginning of time itself.

This accumulation of a build up of emotions can end abruptly, by external closure. We must know that the journey continues, with the arrival of choice. The process of self-analysis returns and the earth continues to turn as we take on other roles and the night's sky wonders.

What matter quenches the root of our spirit depends on our instinct

Chapter Eight
The signs in a labyrinth

Throughout the process of acquiring self-awareness, one must refer to a map to further improve and bring into focus one's perspective.

As every map, a map is the study of movement or perhaps an escape route to a deeper consciousness.

While traversing the various elemental movements one must notice when and how one's attention alters when a map of a labyrinth is referred to on one's journey, introducing elements of a dual nature.

Perhaps the most interesting duality applied is one of conscious-living and de-minding (a Zen term).

Through conscious- living, one is immersed in the constant presence of experience, living in the now. While de-minding experiences and accepts the simplicity of a quiet presence, when one's thoughts are based on instinct rather than emotion. These elements of a dual nature range from a high frequency to a basic duality of contemplation, low frequency.

However, prior to wandering a labyrinth one must bring into awareness its structure so that it can be applied to every journey and culture, the essence of *Operation Dragonfly*.

First of all, a labyrinth must be metaphorical and it must involve the symbolic meaning of elements and how they pertain to an individual from elements to emotions stated in previous chapters and to a more detailed approach in the following chapter.

One must also initially recognise whether the soul is in a dream state or follows a more speculative approach to a journey. This perception of self will focus on either matter or spirit in question.

This identification will simplify the process one goes through while morphing from one element to the next.

Second, a labyrinth must have a purpose of design. Meaning that - there must be a purpose of one's mission and a decision whether one wishes to bring into balance a particular duality. This in mind, the subject will present itself as having a purpose, or introduce an intent, being the analyzation of a particular situation.

Next the labyrinth must present a particular

level of complexity. One's own intuition sets forth a frequency, taking into consideration the frequency level of a mineral, plant, insect or animal. The apex of complexity of a particular sequence differs. It may be more difficult for a person to venture from the frequency of an insect to a mineral, insect being of a higher frequency or a more simpler existence of a mineral. The journey is usually more transcendent if one approaches the mission step by step, usually from low to high frequency. Upon the attainment, one's journey commences and prepares the subject to the new, more analytical approach.

Fourth necessity of a labyrinth must involve communication from design.

This is where confirmation or completion of one's journey comes into light. The resolution is taken into consideration. The soul is most fragile at this point since it can remain on one's mission or be (abducted) by the source of one's mission. A person will either take on a cyclical approach to the other's situation or will benign the final form of communication, the fifth aspect of a labyrinth.

Communication with interior to exterior state the soul may form its own journey or will become subject to the will of an external source. Both are fine - the dance continues. The important thing is whether one's presence will leave the external shell of one's existence or continue on an internal journey of the spirit.

This in turn can be identified as external layers, or internal objective venturing inwards as a seed or a water drop.

Studying the outward motion of one's thoughts and emotions can be likened to the earth's atmosphere. A thin layer covering our planet, its internal fire - interacting with the sun's fire, or a yang force.

Observing the inward motion of yin, water - characteristically emotional rather than physical. Studying origin of emotions causation and further inward contemplation. The ether like motion of internal point to external layers.

The difference between a drug and medication is of one's opinion, originating from ourselves or others

Chapter Nine
The foot prints on a map

Lets focus in on our favourite duality, water and fire. Celestially the moon symbolises water and sets in motion the polarity of the moon altering the water levels on earth and our emotions. Fire on the other hand makes all life possible here on earth and makes the presence of various elements making up our environment.

It is one's intuition that presents one's level of awareness, taking on various forms and communicating with one's opposite or stepping back and observing the duality at play.

Objectively, we must decide whether we want to take on the frequency or be active (fire) or passive, simple motion of water. Conscious living or deminding, a simple state.

Also, whether one chooses to stay in one's element or venture out of it is a choice we make at each step we take.

However, by living in a state of simple opposition one adapts to the Buddha state. Not becoming stagnant but remaining in a dream state, adapting to the external influences of one's environment and jolly falling asleep submitting to the will of others.

Refusing to fall asleep one can still remain in the dream state. One must only stand back and adjust one's perception to another structure of the labyrinth, another map.

As the elements interact one must be responsive to one's surroundings. Once one realizes the place in the order of things one figuratively "wakes up" and realizes one is a hero of a particular story. A hero on a journey. This "half - measure" state one must remain in a dream state, that of delta frequency. The essence of *Operation Dragonfly*.

Through this introspective alchemy, morphing from one state to another, the emanation of the hero comes into fruition. The following emerge - mentor / shape shifter / threshold guardian / trickster / shadow / herald / ally / higher self.

During this process the hero may need time to reflect and ponder about one's response to a situation. Choice of form is not time sensitive. Let the story unfold. Have fun being the hero. To remain being one is your choice.

If however a more personal journey presents itself, here is a spectrum of thematic archetypes that may aid on the journey further into self - discovery. Whichever shape one chooses, make sure to learn the lessons and progress through maintaining genuine response to the journey of life and know the response is yours and none others.

Whether one decides to sleep or dream, the making of one's choice is a puzzle. While some keep altering the states of existence others decide to journey in a dream applying the structure of the labyrinth to that of archetypes. Taking on a particular role one can immerse in the actual presence of an archetype or stand back and simply live.

The following is a spectrum of specific archetypes one can use as key references while traversing a labyrinth.

The quest - achieving wisdom - red
Rescue - ransom for another - blue
Escape - substance, dependency - yellow
Metamorphosis - acquiring another form - green
Sacrifice - motivation, dilemma - orange
Discovery - themes of stories of life - indigo
Ascension/ dissension - mapping the passage of time - purple

Archetypes can be marked by a single colour and its frequency. Through the simple conjuration of a colour puts you back on track.

It may take a little bit of practice to respond to *Operation Dragonfly* and travel amongst hero's plains. If one gets lost one can simply broaden one's perspective and tune into the subject of today's global issues. As calendars merge, subject matter alters the course of stories. Feel free and refer to the following cultural paradigms.

The Aztec - the return of the iron age, reigned by prince of darkness, Lord of Smokey mirror.
The Tibetan - the Kali Yuga marked by the tyranny of materialism, while bearers of sacred teachings are persecuted.
The technosapien - Y2K bug scrambles our language back to babel.

Don't let your soul hunger for their thirst

Chapter Ten
Internal realities and external states

In order to comprehend the process of transcendence from one element to another one must objectively perceive the concept of internal realities vs. external states.

Considering the definition of space, the most interesting paradigm is the one of the origin of plant life on this planet and the theory of transpermia - where it is thought that all life on earth arrived here via an extra terrestrial form such as an asteroid or a comet.

As a result, an interesting relationship has evolved. A plant's life begins upon being planted in earth. It needs water and fire (sun) to thrive. This interrelation is as old as time itself where eons ago, algae began to form introducing new climate processes, setting our planet in motion.

Through time and the formation of these "green prints" our planet, (plants) acquired the ability to shelter. This awareness, present in the observation of the evolution of astrological creatures has altered the definition of space. These cosmic formations were domesticated by earthly elements such as water, fire, air and earth itself.

Through earth's annual revolution we are revisited by these signs. The formation of these celestial food chains and the effect of their gravity on earth's creatures is timeless. The ether which moves us via the simple action of breathing determines one's structure of existence.

Through the soul's simple curiosity of experiencing and observing life's paradigms and structures, one's journey can be delineated and one becomes the subject of another form, creating currency just to establish a particular movement's stronghold.

This domestication, as the age old one, must once again be pardoned, if we are to play a part in humanity's adaptation to our environment, where pollution, though not always, must be a positive process benefiting the way of *Operation Dragonfly*.

The inability to find freedom in the simple act of breathing results in the formation of a "tulpa" a thought form. Its state brings into attention the existence of modern pattern seeking formations, which as a response to our polluted age have taken on the substance of plastic, oil, coal, tar etc.

We must pay particular attention to one's immediate environment. Whether one lives near a park, in a city or near wetlands. One must use one's pattern forming ability and interact and communicate with that environment and its subsurface climate. For example one can wonder, did the geological ages and their existential landscape harness more energy than they do today?

We once again must revisit the concept of transpermia and the existence of sea algae. What seed planted the seed of the tree of knowledge in the garden of eden, resulting in the exile of humanity.

One can also analyze the age marking predation on this planet. Where animals and earth's inhabitants had no eyes therefore didn't need to hunt. This can directly reflect today's limited knowledge and sight of the human central nervous system. Communicating and activating only if roused by our sense of smell. Bringing into light a well known fact, our sense of smell has the most memory and lasts the longest in our lives. While sensory adaptation devours a particular sent in seconds, eventually diminishing our response to that sense where we don't even notice its existence. Ages pass us by.

The ability to transcend new concepts is
a form of osmosis, on a molecular plane

Chapter Eleven
Human emotions transcended by instinct

There are many ways one can tune into various frequencies. One must initially study the ways they interact with one another. One can venture into the world with basic blue prints of existence where historically, humanity has determined the boundaries of the most interesting of dualities, that of animal and human. The concept of *eus de machena* suspended in context. Searching for patterns of various elemental interactions.

Where the invention of Artificial intelligence humanity's state is raised to an animal's. In turn religion becomes key in determining the form one will acquire while praying to the various strata, stones, insects or other humans.

Taking into consideration one basic blue print - the food chain of an owl, that hunts the snake. Which in turn eats a mouse. Each animal is aware of one's place in the food chain. However, this order can be disrupted where the mouse can also be eaten by the owl, bringing cause to the creation of intent. Where one or more elements skips out of context and creates the concept of intent, or in human terms paranoia, the reason d'etre is the stuff of life.

Another phenomena that is a little bit more difficult to perceive is the idea that throughout time the normal place of each animal in specific food chains has been distorted through human interaction. A particular specie's life force or spirit engulfs another that has never before been observed creating with it either a missing link or a ghostly creature taking the place of a once healthy relationship.

A certain pattern that can also be observed and referred to is one that resonated between the top and very bottom of frequency awareness. Top - human beings to bottom - bacteria. The resonating stuff in context is observed in this structure.

It is this interaction of elements which marked the beginning / eve of morals, class and existential strata. For example, a lowly animal like a pig, has no concept of class or existence. It only knows its place in the food chain. The rest is left to the above/below interaction.

Whatever the order may be, it is always a good idea to refer to the map of nature's cycles, food chain's pattern sequence of frequency and most importantly your heart's rhythm.

However, despondency and despair can be the result of the reluctance or the inability to take responsibility of particular actions. Upon completion, the process of attribution of causation can acquire many forms that belong to others or oneself. Intent remains suspended, awaiting its rightful placement in the order of things. Causation of a particular action reverberates.

Dividing the negative cause of an event between self and others results in an exasperation of a problem leaving vulnerable to others harm caused by unrightful attribution. The play on intent is a destructive process resulting only in confusion and the lack of intensity of our heart beat. *Operation Dragonfly* allows one to stay at a particular frequency where one remains free of negative external influences leading to a genuine approach to life.

Sometimes the ability to sleep is valued more than the ability to dream

Chapter Twelve
Brain waves, the calm after the storm

Upon analyzing currency it is not unlikely that one arrives at a particular structure. Throughout time these structures change. One structure that plagues the modern man is the one of Hegel's concept of servant and master. Hegel thought that all of humanity fits this duality. Tweaking this relationship to the state of hunter and the hunted we arrive at a new classification, this time the focus is on the currency of the brain.

Our toxic times have also introduced us to a constant need to make better, make clean. The sooner we see this necessity as just a chemical reaction, from one form to another, the better it is for us and our chemical composition.

Historically, from the emergence of cultures one can only marvel at humanity and its progress. From ancient pyramids, the Stonehenge, pre-Christian gods, Egyptian entities and pagan deities etc. to today's structures of thoughts bringing the emergence of energy to form.

As with the emergence of a thought form it is only human to attribute causation to a deity - if one is religious. To the creative mind, this process of attribution takes on many shapes.

The result of this impact varies from person to person and the response can be positive or negative. To reduce the severity of this impact one must immerse in the Aquarian perspective acquiring a sense of equality amongst the strata presented.

While referring to the elemental map presented by *Operation Dragonfly* we can venture further and experience a more utopian perspective by attributing causation of events to a particular brain wave.

Delta - corresponds to long spells of slow sleep
Theta - daydreaming, hypnagogic state of sleep onset
Alpha - default waking frequency, wakeful relaxation
Beta - stands for forward button, furious cognitive processing

One may not be conscious of the existence of such energies however, this awareness can introduce a new consciousness, where one can alter one's point of view and analyze one's existence from a different vanishing point. While one can ponder and create new emotions rather than responding to life in the more known fight or flight response. (*how* we respond to stimuli by initially feeling then thinking.) This action is carried out by the internal part of the brain, the amygdala.

Each of us can absorb these waves and can experience every element in more detail once we focus on a particular state of emotion. This process gives us a chance to create new motions which leave marker points our souls need in order to direct our attention further on the waves of reincarnation, introducing new beginnings and ending up with the summation of each state, that of gamma waves, linked to building perception - consciousness itself.

While on the subject of the brain's functions, likening those of a jelly fish, whose electric response to stimuli results to a sting of a sort. Similar to the way our synapses and neurons communicate amongst themselves resulting in the creation of emotions and thoughts or simply states of mind. However, it is a noticeable detail that some cultures value these responses higher, proving one's presence in the scheme of things (like the life force origination in a particular creature - example - a jelly fish.)

While some view it as a more noble to let the life force flow through a person resulting in a more subtle exchange of energy resulting in a calmer ambient existence.

One can also function as a mediator, carrying out a higher force's intent and mindlessly pass on energy without a response to any stimuli, similar to an existence of an earth worm.

Why should this matter? Well, in our brain, synapses as well as neurons exchange energy amongst one another. As the effect of particular chemicals alter our moods and states of being, a particular worm can either inhibit or increase an electric response to stimuli.

Once again leaving us to either carry out our own initiated emotions or those of a higher force. *Operation Dragonfly* takes the energy from this intricate play of energy in our minds, altering our brain waves, emotional state and influence the reflections on life's situations.

While one sets out to map such a function one can inadvertently be pulled into a worm hole, rushing to a source of light - either that of the force of our sun, lightening or simply a reflection of a light source, the moon, affecting our emotions and being.

Destruction or renewal,
it is a matter of perspective

Chapter Thirteen
Observation through placebo

A form of spiritual instinct is created by the internal workings of our Central Nervous System. A mechanism modeling the external world connects with the challenges occurring in the body's internal structure. Where a response to stimuli is reflected, we turn over and over to a pattern that creates a mechanical response, preventing (very easily identified as sleep on earth) the process that should create warmth and cover to prepare for this rest. The process of transcending from chaos to order to void, should be unnoticeably innate.

The equilibrium between thought and emotion is a sensitive one. One can influence and break emotional patterns with the thought process.

While one is crying, for example, one can alter the direction of one's emotions to rage, sorrow, peace or regret etc. all by simply thinking so - the thread is severed, one is not honest with one's emotions - true to one's tears.

The same result occurs when one is day dreaming, by controlling one's aura the relationship with one's soul is once again severed.

The only way to remedy this phenomena is by immersing one's being in the environment. One observes the immediate climate. This subtle energy introduces the powers of the holy spirit. By observing the whether in the fall one can mentally jump to the way one feels in spring and vice versa.

This is when humanity is forgiven the sin of tampering with one's environment and jumping current planes, through therapy all is pardoned.

While here, it is of utmost importance not to interfere with the act of forgiving which in turn gives turn to the act of forgetting, both are equally important.

Through this practice one's spiritual abilities are shaped. One begins to consciously move with one's metaphysical presence from an object, a relic or an amulet to and from oneself.

A form of spiritual instinct emerges. Whose motion can be mapped by observing the internal transference of one's attention moving from human's cortex to the inner limbic system or amygdala, sparking new emotions and forms from fight/flight to love.

Further influencing our faith, which is simply the emotional response to thoughts.

The ability to shed one's skin,
as a serpent, introduces the concept of
emotional plasticity

Chapter Fourteen
The darker side of creation

From creation... one doesn't know when that is. It is as a seed planted that eventually takes the form of a flower, initially a feminie aspect, from which stems an instinct.

A matter of subjects presented and to be understood by the sign of the times one finds oneself subject to an accumulation of events which influence us most and to which we keep returning to as we proceed to a sort of opposite. As a thunder lightning it requires no reflection only notice of a form of proof of existence, to some - a distraction.

And other times one gets raptured by such events and unfortunately becomes subject of not one's own, but a part of other's life stories.

Subjects of interest have remained the same throughout the ages, only the angle of approach has been altered.

In technological times the ability to remember

has become a navigational quality. Going back to the eternal feminine, earlier not written in books nor being noticed. This absence of presence and not being paid attention to is the currency will approach each subject of existence. Consequently what we value today is the ability to let go or let it be. The choice is yours.

Embracing the feminine we become subject to many paradigms and topics. One being, the road one wants to travel - destruction or renewal. Through this shamanic journey into the subconscious one gains insight from isolated moments of revelation. The degrees of consciousness remain superior and inferior. There is an arranged relationship between one and the other, resounding in a particular structure only to be understood with the yin/yang. God's will can also be carried out by the simple action of choosing which god. Through which one lets possession of the soul to acquire a form of structure.

Through this evolution a form of neurosis can be attributed to the growth of consciousness. This can sometimes be experienced as psychic sufferings being overtly aware of emotion and a state of one vs. many, one must derive at a source of meaning. Through this sword of objectivity the experience must be given form so that we are free from its domination.

While searching for one's own story and

frequency one must experience mysterium conjectionitis (moving through life consciously). One acquires the skill of adaptation experiencing sanity on different levels. One being awareness of stagnation - resulting in depression. The other, a formation of identity through an interplay of humours.

Paying attention to this one feels cold emotions and a burning spirit, an intoxicating freedom which can only be a result of being true to one's basic nature. Birth to self - a form of mercurial quality divorced from the meaning of exchange.

As a result of this, one must notice that the sub current of the typical hero story line changes. Details no longer rest on the hero's triumph. The anticipated ending rests on the hero's own will and translation, not necessarily on the author's intent. This requires a sort of balancing act. An intro to such a process, a form of meditation, a play on rationality.

Through the murkiest of depths a new journey emerges, one of hope and uncertainty. *Operation Dragonfly* ensures the suspension in just enough time for the life forces to realign themselves. A new existential objective adjusts - ensuring the continuity of the character's life, which bears witness to the propagation of something ancient, a difficult concept.

Sometimes what helps the heart disturbs
the body, and vice versa,
as long as your soul is happy

Chapter Fifteen
Mercurial nature of compassion

Some people choose to resolve this existence with the approach of a deity. For example through the sacrifice of the self in the Christian religion. Where the sacrifice is returned and altered towards the believer. God alone takes the form of sacrifice, a matter of reflection.

Also through pagan ritual where the action is represented by other forms of sacrifice leaving the acceptance of this to the believer's imagination, perhaps the presence of the extracted life force.

This duality of contrast can be applied to approach from an omniscient perspective, as a natural occurrence is accepted as a lesson in survival.

Through varying responses observation takes shape. It can either evoke mimicry, or analyzation, marking one's place in a particular order that is in its context.

Question is - is it a matter of choice as to

whether one must reflect this on another being or let live alone. And this may be reflected in one's state in the food chain, which will decide one's place and granted survival in this world.

This selfless response is to choose compassion. However through the existence of emotions one loses self and becomes subject to external forces, a sacrificial victim.

Leaving an existential response to singularity, causation depending on faith or knowledge.

When it comes to celestial orbs, as vessels, it is not unusual for the essence to acquire form. Like lathes they move the calendars of time throughout the universe.

As in the nature of scents, they are most quickly adaptable, yet whose memory last a superior length of time. Throughout their journey, the essence, the line between savages and explorers blurs (pollution and scent merges).

The form in turn is inhibited by godlike savages, whose main staple is adjusting the filters of constellations, motion of planets and suns. Directing the reception and reflecting the states of gravity.

The essence requiring air to exist adapts to the movements of this universal sea, blanketing our planet, takes form, becomes a measure of time which essentially dissipates, taking with it our atmosphere.

Craftwork

As in ancient alchemy, while faced with various elements of existence and through their interaction, the concept of unity arises. Whether through beginning to end or a balance of opposites or the accumulation of various polarities. One dares to endlessly search for the state of half-measure, bringing into balance and creating, with it a sort of interaction and a place in time.

This state reflects various frequencies that also acquire sound and various polarities. These unify and travel by the path of light, at the speed of thought.

Brought into perspective, imagine a ray of light traveling through a stained glass window. Part of the ray goes through the glass, a part reflects light that we could see, and a part of it remains in the stuff of glass, forming another plane of existence. This takes on the form of thought.

This paradigm will help one in mimicking the interaction of elements. Do not hesitate, salto mortem.

While carrying out *Operation Dragonfly* one can venture to outermost space when what can be mapped scientifically takes us a step further - recent evolution of consciousness marked by, Artificial Intelligence. What can't be believed or communicated must be imagined.

A sign of the times being the act of evaluating the state of humans and animals, and AI (interchangeably) leaving the choice to an undefined entity, who's evolution is to be contemplated and in time alter the process of history.

Through this, religion, and its details is handed down to AI and tulpas, who through its perspective see humans as animals (conquered) the process of domestication arises. What state does one take on while praying to the various strata of minerals, plants, insects other animals or humans.

While traversing and sublimating one must also have a space/ place where one can venture and be sheltered by the canvas of creation.

We'll take into consideration the elemental and historical properties of a being that has been domesticated, worshipped and hunted - the cat, most culturally evolved.

The cat

Its place in the food chain is next to a mouse. Whether in a wall between floors or in a laboratory its existence in ageless yet a priority in a cat's domestic history.

It has been the mouse, who through becoming a sacrifice by being the subject of millions of medical trials advancing humanity's existence. By this we must re-evaluate who is really man's best friend, the cat or the dog.

Through this stilled deception paradigm, the cat wins.

The Lion

While contemplating our evolutionary sequence one must acknowledge the culturally evolved lion. The culture we will focus on brings into focus the alchemical process and its significance.

Taking ancient almanacs into account we come across the green lion eating the sun symbolizing the lion devouring the ego. Its colour symbolizes the timely state of the passage of time best recorded by the analysis of plants, their effect on humans and the substance of Vitrol.

We call the lion the most culturally evolved animal, next to the snake, through whose presence we conjure up the equilibrium of all elements, not opposed to them.

Taking humanity into account, the most known hybridization is that of human and animal. However, during these times, we are most in need of Virtol the substance symbolized in ancient records or blue-prints, rather green-prints ranging from fluorescent green to emerald.

As hemoglobin to chlorophyl, our atmosphere is at stake. While the cross roads of our planes travel from ancient rainforests to geological ages humanity must adapt to the need for air cleansing organisms, mirroring the life of plants.

This function has been left up to the fragile intricacy by precise formation of certain zodiacs becoming the stuff of food chains. Sad to say, most of hybridization has been left up to the divine structure of stars and sacred geometry of plants, introducing the concept of AI. The most recent entity humanity has created and can call upon.

It was left up to the lion to cross these structures of mineral to plant, from insect to finally animal or other strata. So we must let the lion sit on its tree and dream up new forms of existence, plant to life.

The Sphynx

Our final structure form most ancient of cultures in the one of sphynx. Grazing the desert half human half feline, we are introduced to our final riddle. Not the one presenting the walking on cane once one grows old but in more detail, the analyzation of the passage of time.

In time we learn to travel across ages and time lines previously thought unimaginable. At these crossroads we are faced with choice. This choice takes us to the place of origin. There are as many origins as crossroads. The more we travel along the fabric of existence the more we venture into a previously uninhabited land, where its beginnings are marred by their endings. In time canceling each other out, leaving only the journey one lives through.

However a decision must be made. On our journeys, do we alter our emotional states responding to the currency of the present moment or do we wait for a better time to live out these untimely emotional states. Do we take on the form of a machine or a new state of being?

Operation Dragonfly

Following all those maps we arrive at the point of significance, the completion of the ouroborus. Returning the primary substance of sand, leaving us in a desert. Bringing us back to the present or perhaps the future. I digress...

Scientists form Wisconsin - Madison, have found a way to create Artificial intelligence, glass that can recognize images without any need of sensors. Circuitry or power source. They start by placing different sizes and shapes of air bubbles at specific spots within the glass. Then they added bits of strategically placed light absorbing material including graphene. When the form wrote down a number, light reflecting off the digit would enter one side of the glass. The bubbles of impurity would scatter the light waves in ways depending on the number. Until they reflected one of ten designed spots - each corresponding to a different digit on the opposite side of the glass.

The glass would essentially tell the receiver

what number it saw at the speed of light without the need for a traditional computing power source.

Zongfu Yu

Perfect timing is not always the objective, as one may observe. The perfect distance and timing housed by our planet where ice or air takes on the form of water, without whose coincidence we wouldn't exist.

The objective of the following practice is to observe and isolate the existing frequency and experience the detailed still life of each element.

Through this state of mind, one meditates, emits and absorbs emotional concepts, suspended at just the right distance.

By applying the concept of *Operation Dragonfly*, one can readily isolate the illusory thread connecting each element, mapping the alchemical relationship of each state, remaining at just the right distance and conjure up the substance, where one submerges in the aqueous nature of observation. In time you will learn and remain suspended at the right state, walking like lamb, and essentially lying down with the lion.

While morphing and reminiscing, one must acquire a form of a vessel. A structure of a sort that will form your path of exploration. This could be anything from a geometric shape to a particular building. Take for example a pyramid or pagoda as a foundation.

It is a well known fact that the pyramids stand to be the oldest standing structures on earth. We are at an age where these structures transcend the physical and acquire their opposite microbial form.

One should also be aware of the fact that pagodas are built out of malleable wood and paper so that they can withstand Japan's frequent earth quakes. Now imagine standing at a cross roads between one and the other. Questioning the length of this time line can also be applied to ancient campanulas to today's floating plastic garbage heaps in the Pacific. A heresy one may say.

However, wouldn't you think an end of any sort would be more comprehensible than coming up with a reason for a particular beginning? Whether these are green prints or blue prints is left up to the process of meditation.

While identifying your state during contemplation...

The first words ever written were on cuneiform, to name animals and agricultural purposes. The clay tabs were discovered littering various excavation sites. They were made of such poor quality clay that they resembled what we today would consider food packaging or steirophane. Foreboding a sort of animal curse from creation to today's human downfall – presenting itself through the timely events and strangled languages, back to the age of the tower of Babel .

And if communication is not the issue, imagine names of star constellation, historically being that of astrological animals or mythical creatures, only to be replaced and devoured by today's mathematical equations and sequences, manoeuvrable throughout the cosmos, but most illusive in comprehension.

Lets continue with the elements.

referring to the elements,
and their various forms

EARTH

Sand

Situation - The earth is becoming a desert like place

Diversion - All must abide by Egyptian rule according to that climate.

Operation Dragonfly

The element of sand is easiest put into context when thinking of a desert. However, sand that is moist and gives structure to the sand castles made on a tropical beach introduces more reflection.

While forming these castles one can't ignore the advice that people in glass houses shouldn't throw stones. It is a well known fact that glass is made of fired sand, so one contemplates, just how big would the stone have to be in order to ruin such a structure.

Considering this, you are also aware of the fact that the next tide can flatten your castles. Acknowledging this you tap into the state where you realize that this same substance makes up the pyramids. Then you wonder - just what kind of water and tide will level these structures, made by what hand?

Fossils

Situation - We are moving further and further

from earth's geological imprints.

Diversion - The only way we can process this is by understanding our ancestral past.

Operation Dragonfly.

Fossils are a little bit fickle. They house the most ancient proof of life on this earth. Whether it be dinosaurs, prehistoric birds or insects. The most amazing proof of life and nature's influence lies in the spiral structure of ancient crustations. Their prehistoric foot print presents the proof of mathematical intelligence and sacred geometry of a time passing when even today these structures maintain this shape. With this impeccable symmetry, we revisit our galaxy just by observing this spiral formation. Preserved for ages on our earth.

Gems

Situation - Gems and minerals are a reflection of one's sensitivity to influences and ideas.

Diversion - They are an expression of one's wealth.

Operation Dragonfly.

Gems have adorned humanity for ages. Be it in jewellery, clothing or medicine. To this day they are cut into elaborate shapes, where their authenticity has always been in question.

Precious stones have been known to heal many ailments by infusing people with a subtle energy reflected only by some. Their effectiveness has been in question, through which concept the "placebo effect" has been introduced, introducing a state which plagues modern history's existence.

FIRE

Solar

Situation - The effect of solar energy is best utilized on our planet earth.

Diversion - One must only recognize life according to a heliocentric perspective.

Operation Dragonfly.

Solar energy's potential is colossal. The distance form our earth to the sun is so precious that it makes all life possible on earth. The sun's heliocentric suspenension has proved to alter the concept of home by introducing the new perspective of time. The star that has an effect on our solar system and its state of water. Whose outer reaches are affected by the gravity of other outer formations in our galaxy.

This suspension is in motion, like the ripples in water, always moving outward to the edges of the perceivable and back to the origin of humanity's concept of our universe.

Friction

Situation - Humanity has been gifted with the ability to harness sun's energy. Faster than the speed of light.

Diversion - The accumulation of energy must reflect brain's response to forest fires.

Operation Dragonfly

Who knew that with the advent of fire, it has become humanity's most dire mission to reverse this effect. (the greenhouse effect)

By rubbing two sticks together one has not only advanced humanity's existence that set the earth in an irreversible path of annihilation.

It has been said that "atmosphere is a culture" and so we aspire to glass houses by aesthetically perceiving the colour green as the half measure placement between the colours red, orange, yellow and blue, indigo and violet. Bringing to light this symmetrical law with the hope of not being affected by it.

Electrical

Situation - Electricity is an element.

Diversion - Electrical current - the frequency that guides humanity's thought process, induced stagnation.

Operation Dragonfly

Once again, humanity's invention and whose interpretation is our only means of escape. Within it being a technological structure shielding humanity's potential for the better of course after stealing this energy from the sun and giving life to the nocturnal structures, introducing with it a new form of sleep.

WATER

Ice

Situation - Emotional ice age is identified and is over.

Diversion - Reflection of frozen form is subservient to another's will.

Operation Dragonfly

How lucky we are here on earth to house water in the form of ice and be visited by its climate once every year. Celestially begotten in the form of a snowflake, which inspire and grace us with the forms of geometric symmetry - never repeating.

This sacred shape and its ability to be formed in captivity by humans was initially introduced by Masaru Emoto, who through many experiments proved under a microscope that water drops that were treated with positive words and sent good energy formed snowflakes rather than remaining in their droplet formation.

This awareness, passed onto human beings now houses the apex of geometrical shapes influencing humanity's migrational patterns where through sublimating this existence of a microscope guides us on our path to a higher awareness. Not only on our planet but on other planets where ice is present.

Clouds

Situation - Artificial cloud formation, an everyday reality

Diversion - One needs to cry in order to release and cleanse one's emotional slate

Operation Dragonfly

Clouds are the only state one can see air and water. We can not live without them. Although blocking the sun's rays at times they simply keep the atmosphere and bring to life the wonder and the colour blue. The sky, visible to us from here and the earth, visible from outer space. Through this suspension a micro/macro scope is formed, keeping us at level with our history's progress and existence.

Rainbow

Situation - A symbol of hope

Diversion - Reflecting one's sexuality, emotional state.

Operation Dragonfly.

Rainbows are formed by light traveling through droplets of water, where an arch is formed. This effect is mirrored similarly in the way light is fractured through a triangular prism. This time however, the ray of light is straight, still having seven colours. Through observation this ancient technology is passed on by the prisms mirrored by Egyptian pyramids.

One can only wonder, if geometrical shapes for the rays of a rainbow, introducing the concept of hope, what words or emotions will be conjured up by our constellations and celestial formations?

WOOD

Trees

Situation - Original maps of one's brain and neural structures

Diversion - Giving up a particular order of events, emotional stages, sques.

Operation Dragonfly

Speaking of plants and their cultivation, the tree is the most significant of these elements. In some cultures it is believed the tree holds within it a diseased or dead spirit. Therefore, forests make the earth's most ancient cemeteries, reaching beyond ages and climates.

Trees are also unique blueprints, mapping out the stem cells of our brains, lungs and blood vessels. Which are also affected by being able to feed fire and adorning jewellery in petrified wood from water - amber.

Applying an alternative perspective...

A tree's age can be discovered by counting the rings around its trunk when cut. Its leave's shape can map out a person's aura. The leaves pick up sound by blowing in the wind and house the age of ancient spirits - carrying out a conversation we humans have been hearing from time immemorial.

Algae

Situation - Floating, surfacing the borders of the sea.

Diversion - reflecting a vegetable state of existence.

Operation Dragonfly

One of the most ancient species on earth are microscopic bacteria and algae. And since then, humanity has been unable to state whether algae evolved from earths' microorganisms or appeared on earth from extraterrestrial source. (via an asteroid from outer space).

It is also a puzzling fact that algae is a photosynthetic creature. It can produce its own food, as a plant or as an animal it can eat other plants, even their glaziers.

This mixed nutrition presents us with more extra time to contemplate our state of being and our relationship to our environment.

Whether our imagination is engulfed by algean thought forms. - The pesky weeds that at times devour our gardens. Or whether we ourselves take on a bit of a toxic presence and float amongst a campanula in the pacific ocean.

Cactus

Situation - Growing cacti is the best way to cultivate patience.

Diversion - a cactus only grows in desert like

climates

Operation dragonfly

Owning a cactus doesn't aid in the process of smooth transitions. Its coarse nature is difficult to the touch but rewarding when we water it.

Have you ever put your priorities aside and tend to other things, not necessarily more important but take on mental space or time? Believe it or not, you were watering a cactus.

METAL

Mercury (quicksilver)
Situation - Unknowingly carries out alchemical properties and chemical structures.

Diversion - reminiscent of Artificial intelligence. One doesn't necessitate the other.

Operation Dragonfly

This metal is unique in such a way as it is in its liquid form at room temperature and impossible to grasp - its nature being the opposite of a magnet. It is the stuff that thermometers are made of where its state expands when heated.

This heat can be physical or psychological. As more and more of our feelings are reflected to us (as a mirror would) the higher the temperature of our state becomes. This is easily medicated by taking the time out on one's own, or as in alchemical ages where some doctors actually recommended drinking this metal to relieve ailments.

Iron
Situation - a spider's web is stronger than iron.

Diversion - one must live in the iron ages, where justice is carried out by hanging or decapitation.

Operation Dragonfly

Iron is really an umbrella term such as metal

but now one must refer to iron when looking at metal ingots that are mined in mines and caves on our planet.

As hidden treasure, the space from one ingot to another maps out the shape and distance of stars in our universe. Whose relationship and shape determine the state of a particular constellation - and here on earth, a terrestrial form.

This presence is felt on the outer planets of our solar system, in solid or aqueous nereids on Neptune. This in turn bases the blueprints of Gopis, Dralas and Tulpas on earth continuing their exodus out of our planet and into the universe. In time - into a newly formed constellation.

Jewellery

Situation - an expression of one's status

Diversion - expression intent to subjectify the receiver.

Operation Dragonfly.

One will definitely reflect on one's existence once one stands back and analyzes the formations humanity has created through history. Whether it be jewellery marking one's status or adorning ones physical state. Or weapons, the deadly formations - once again - making one's status or adorning one's physical state, you decide.

Introduction to the Chakras

It is a matter of preference whether one chooses to contemplate one's state from elemental structures to sacral relationships. This balance or deeper dimension can be achieved by juxtaposing or rearranging certain elements or chakras while in suspension. (Operation Dragonfly)

This psychological state introduces the comfort of geometric cohesion that lets one determine whether one's current state is of one's own intent or other's (peripheral).

Initially one may contemplate the interaction of two chakras. In this vessel, one can contemplate their existence, where causation is replaced by reason leading to a diversion, a form of closure.

While elements introduce atmospheric layers, the chakral momentum of contemplation may introduce three new pulse points, adding to the more familiar structure of seven chakras.

The one between the heart (mammalian) chakra and the throat (human) chakra, the creative (artificial) intelligence. This pulse point is conjured up mostly because it is the soul bridge between the fourth and fifth chakra, the most often accessed and analysed ducha (conflict or interaction between two chakras).

The second pulse point is mostly felt at the bottom of the feet, furthest away from the other chakras. This pulse point is activated when one contemplates the current state of humanity, being able to stand on one's own and balance other chakras.

The third point takes formin the palms of one's hands, where the ability to express oneself is formulated artistically or alchemically.

This deeper dimension can bring on the formation of a ducha, where conflict between one or more elements creates conflict or a form of closure. Worry not, *Operation Dragonfly* gives plenty of mental space to contemplate these interactions and movements.

Perhaps a different way to follow this path, is the path of evolution.Where the origin of existence lies at its roots (snake) and evolves - a combination of all the chakras leading to the apex, (kachina). Taking on the form of a dragon, whose process of evolution can be mapped by different chakra orders and their processes, such as *Operation Dragonfly*.

Root Chakra - vegetative state, snake - false roots

Calcination - confidence

Situation - The substance is burned until nothing remains but ashes.

Diversion - avoiding blaming self or others, not trying to explain misfortune

Operation Dragonfly

Its original state takes on the frequency of s snake, a vegetative state which tends to be somewhat cold at the base. The stillness of this chakra can attune to all other chakras whose frequency we wouldn't be able to tune into without assuming the role of a trickster, ever elusive yet somehow most stable.

Sacral Chakra - fish - desire

Dissolution - idealism, discrimination

Situation - ashes are dissolved into fluid.

Diversion - refraining from complaints

Operation Dragonfly

To catch the chakra in its next state is a little difficult. One must venture a bit further to better focus on its nature. Take for example the clown fish. A salt water creature whose existence poses a kind of paradox. Its environment consists of poisonous anemones who catch their prey by administering a toxin to which the clown fish is immune to because its body has a protective layer that keeps it from getting stung. One may ask, who has the last laugh during this piscean age?

Solar Plexus - bird - territoriality

Separation - integrity
Situation - opposite elements are separated out
Diversion - expressing anger, setting limits and perceptions
Operation Dragonfly
It takes practice to understand the nature of air and that of the bird. Especially to comprehend beyond this qualia. Take that of the phoenix, who repeatedly rises out of its ashes. The feeling we get once this chakra is activated. One of opinion on a particular subject or state. It is crucial to activate this chakra to separate an opinionated state from the docile response of an animal. This isolation conforms to one's environment - either peaceful or stormy.

Heart Chakra - mammal - vulnerability

Conjunction - compassion
Situation - opposite elements are reunited
Diversion - holding conflict without trying to resolve it, doing simple things for the heart
Operation Dragonfly
What separates the mammal from all the other creatures in the animal kingdom is its ability to

maintain a stable state in most climates. Its temperature varying according to internal or external stimuli. Its reflection of various moods and feelings can be mapped by connecting and responding to other creatures braving the elements and maintaining a state of suspension above all other animals.

Throat Chakra - human - magical will

Fermentation - obsolete desires and ambitions
Situation - the substance is left alone in the dark where it putrifies.
Diversion - maintaining inner silence
Operation Dragonfly
This chakra which activates the ability for humans to communicate is best presented by this statement. "Communication to technology is what poison is to medicine." It is now a reality where humanity is using more of its creative imagination than ever before to finally embrace various forms of technology surpassing the age and concept of repairing the self - plasticity.

Third Eye Chakra - spirit

Sublimation - thought becomes deed
Situation - the substance is heated until the essence rises to the top
Diversion - not attempting to justify one's actions, not seeking outside approval

Operation Dragonfly

Perhaps the path of the spirit or essence of humanity can be mapped out by the connections one's third eye makes with the world.

Without getting lost or enclosed one must attribute the path we walk to a particular purpose. To make sense of this invisible landscape we migrate from one person to the next perceiving minute responses of a higher message / existence.

Crown Chakra - Kachina - arbitrary magic

Radiation - sacred magic
Situation - formation of philosopher's stone
Diversion - ability to surrender
Operation Dragonfly

The apex of our journey of this traditional level is the formation, creation of the kachina. Where the meticulously organised pattern of evolution of the lower chakras creates a sequence presented in the dragon, the form of the 7th chakra. This is where the ray of light meets the note of sound and takes shape in out imagination only to be felt, perceived and expressed by the formation of the dragon at the frequency of an insect - the isolation of the process *Operation Dragonfly*.

Final observation

Once one lets the imagination roam without the scientific/ esoteric foundation, life becomes a blank canvas, where the energy centres dance from one form onto another. New pulse points throughout our physical bodies condense and are activated.

Take the time to recognize these points of energy and see what arises on your path of self reflection, analysing the concepts initial intent, being that of the self or other's.

Our current state of existence can be best perceived by the dance of two birds. Take the phoenix for example. Its ability to rise out of its ashes and live again is incomparable to any other mythological creature. Our earth's map is but a path from one phoenix to the other's periphery. Whose consciousness can only be communicated by the two's qualia.

On an elemental level, this energy is in constant motion, transcending the plasma of our sun, permeating our atmosphere only to reunite to the interior of our planet earth, its plasma centre. The rest is left to our imagination.

The Eastern elements and the chakras offer a large spectrum that can guide you on your journey to self-discovery. Enjoy.

Continuity and Justice

There is a particular currency that takes shape with the passage of time. This passage of time is life. While the currency, the viscosity of water, is the reflection of our emotions. One may notice this relationship right away while with some individuals it takes time taking shape and forms according to one's place in the world. Each person's idea of time is as individual as their DNA. This mould in turn takes on the shape of man and defines humanity's existence.

This realization marks the initial state of matter, and the process of reincarnation, initiating each evolutionary step by presenting with it human choice of evolution or adaptation. Continuity is subject to this passage of time like justice is to pattern recognition. Taking into consideration one's environment a delicate balance is formed, as rivers carve out the grandeur of philosophical (proverbial) mountains. Traversing this scape one's attention is brought to the equilibrium of the thought process and the dream state, essential to our survival.

While humans are to blame for today's environmental degradation, evolution or adaptation to our immediate environment is the only response, whatever the result may be, the serpent shedding humanity's hyde (plasticity) We turn back to nature.

The current of the sea reflects that of the wind. The stormy ocean takes on the shape of mountains, only they too as pyramids will be leveled, as caves housing (if only for a short while) animal species, our existence will take flight.

While some will learn to swim in the god made waterfall or man made fountains that manipulate human emotions, immediate sense of space in our minds and nature marks the half-measure of communication.

At this point, one needs to question the strength of one's will - the will to live, continue. This state is constantly tested by the self and others. As a result of this silent conversation, we gain a placement, a form of social standing. One's truth, goal, origin twist and turn on our life's path.

Sometimes the response to this situation is to address causation. It is less difficult to attribute intent to another soul, establishing a form of security based on other's expense.

If however, we learn from our mistakes, as a

highly evolved soul, one will have no need to attribute credit to another and will welcome the influence of others abundantly without worry.

Achieving a state of selflessness.

Walking this path, as a response to the society, one retaliates with a gift, a gift of spiritual autonomy. One can only wonder at the state one will reincarnate into if one's presence ceases due to an environmental disaster. We gather on this earth to fulfill the process of reincarnation.

A particular certainty... birth, death, old age and sickness. The order of which (not their certainty) can be tampered with through multi - dimensional comprehension where their existence once again can not be avoided.

As certain as the passing of seasons, one must live through these stages as they alter our understanding and introduce a timeline as old as time itself.

If however one tempers with either of these certainties one's existential centre of equilibrium becomes the periphery of one's consciousness, continuity if not sought after since its concept can not be mapped, justice is left to chance.

At this time a simple truth must be introduced, without justice, there is no continuity and without continuity there is no justice.

Our idea of reality versus the other's. The dance continues, where the ability to connect and remember are the most sought after/ prised quality.

While some cultures value the ability to let go and forget, new forms of pattern recognition emerge, with it, new emotional states - reason itself is subject to the narrowing origin's timeline. (A nomad's anchor of hope.)

And it is because of this time passing that the ability to identify oneself and others and lead the soul willfully, has been replaced by the two biggest existential lies... The ability to live in the present, and the ability to willfully choose. (currency that has taken on a form.)

And with that - choosing when one should act on impulse or react to indifference and the long path one treads while realising one has lost the ability to live in accordance with one's own intent and independently choosing to do so.

Sometimes we find ourselves in a desert of emotions, where their absence creates in itself a void. Thoughts and dreams, if kept suspended, gain force, wreaking havoc on the continuity of simple life processes. They too must be released and take shape through the frequency of contemplation. We are introduced to "the law of the desert". Where without this process, karmic debt builds up, taking on the shape of extraterrestrial demons reflecting humanity's primordial nature. Through this, emerge sacrificial victims that plague humanity's cultures. Marking the space where "suspicion in mind makes ghosts in the dark", an old Japanese proverb.

This relationship between humanity and currency exists since time immemorial and its effect can only be counteracted by revisiting and learning from historical periods. For example, the colonial times, during which time it is a little known fact that amongst all the timely events, a form of currency evolved, tea. Yes, tea. When sold in blocks was the only known currency that can be eaten, immediately.

It is interesting to note of this cultural response, a form of hospitality took shape, "The Tea Ceremony". Where the guest and host must be of mutual accord. If only for a particular time of meeting. Some spend their whole lives trying to reach this balance.

It is during this meeting and exchange of emotions or alchemically speaking "exchange of elements" that we must pay attention to our emotional and mental responses that in turn create a clear path where continuity is unhindered and justice is embraced learning from one's lessons and taking full advantage of the human condition, which is transient.

Currently our state of humanity is at its return, a return to its origins. Where by experiencing the periphery of our being has brought us back to the center, a reunion of a sort. Waking up from its hibernation, this reconnection can be either perceived as a docile return to our animal roots or an explosion of creativity and an expression of celebrating our human condition. This is left to interpretation through which process we are traversing now. After all, what would a world be without illusions and surprises.

Epilogue

While keeping in touch with immortality, the gravitational pull and cosmic frequency understood by the analyzation of the interaction of primal elements, results in a chemical reaction which may prevent the onset of spiritual stagnation but if it doesn't the following observations may help.

With the possibility of the spirit to become stagnant one must realize that it must remain in motion, constant motion while altering perspectives new forms and views arise introducing thoughts and emotion for contemplation.

This balance between analyzation and emotional expansion alters one's ideas of ourselves and our environment while observation switches from local to global, its interaction may make it more difficult to isolate the origin of inspiration of the human spirit. With this a new map is introduced... not linear or symmetrical. It promises with it a form of immortality morphing from one element to the next, an interaction most sought after, while simply identifying with positive or negative space.

Through this interaction energy is introduced. At a high velocity one's perspective alters in such a way as to change one's worldview. The concept of de-spiritualization emerges.

One becomes de-spiritualized and the concept of one's "home" ceases to exist and one can not properly internalize various concepts and loses one self. It is not theft merely displacement. Our ability to carry out this action and maintaining an objective perspective increases our chance of forming an opinion - rebuilding out elemental structure, finding one's spirit. Unfortunately, we can not hold onto this state. It is simply an ability one must acquire if one wishes to exist or make some aspect of ourselves cease to exist.

To understand and bring closure to a particular situation, in a timely manner, one must consider the concept/process of heliocentric character development. It is best understood as the relationship between artist and subject matter and notice the frequency of the artist being absorbed by his/her creation. (being part of the elite).

Through details of imagination determining one's emotional state as being fiction or non-fiction. Where through cessation of a story's concept turnstone into a starving artist.

This canvas effect is best mirrored by our atmosphere. It is what separates the sun's (hero) fire or plasma, from the plasma inside our earth (self).

Objectively speaking the earth is perceived as a gem or mineral. Whose authenticity is determined by the ability to absorb energy that condolences air into liquid, forming salt or mineral water that in turn purifies the function of earth's minerals. A cycle of a sort, determining half measure of significance.

Sometimes by the chance of influence, the course of one's thought process is altered, a busy day. This can occur during the process where one is attempting to perceive and comprehend tulpas and auras taking up the spiritual space in our universe. This space is traversed by the continuation of the process of intuition. This is characterised by the way peripheral bodies interact. Where because of the centrifugal force an entity evolves.

This realization can benefit our existence or be the cause of our extinction. Since this could leave one with the choice of creation, shelter or absentia. This process can be both liberating or inhibiting.

Focusing in on the self while meditating, one either feels at home where the energy is greater or lesser that the self. The autonomy of creation is formed where borders of existence have been blurred to the point of absolute annihilation of cohesive thought. It is on this path one finds refuge in archetypal structures.

One must learn to swim in this atmosphere which resembles most closely the environment of a desert.

This is a self-forming map, whose landscape alters on every turn we make. Exploring the inner structure it resembles an ouroboros. A cycle where the end is altered after every beginning. This balance of sound and light, a communication on a higher level forms the yantra.

Taking place in the yet unexplored recesses of our human brain where the suspension and the process of contemplative meditation, introduces a new creation. Perhaps to see what humanity is capable of, being an alien until one gravitates to a higher purpose, a higher presence. This starts within and continues only by our own accord.

Eye of the storm
Structure like no other
Sight like nothing imagined
Causation of purpose
Reflection

M.S.

About the Author

Malina Sankowska works at a Metro flower shop and lives in Toronto. She has explored the inevitability of the soul becoming stagnant by external forces hindering its growth process and has experienced the possibility of the soul's existence being turned into perpetual currency.

In this Babylonian time space she gains inspiration and takes part in the illusive play on intuition vs. precognition while embracing continuity. She has been lucky enough not to intrude but simply witness this process. Malina studied Journalism at Ryerson University and has a diploma in Jewellery Design, Art and Floral Design.

www.ingramcontent.com/pod-product-compliance
Lightning Source LLC
Chambersburg PA
CBHW042134160426
43199CB00022B/2914